TRAPPER'S MOON

By

Jim Hunter

With a foreword by Pierson F. Melcher

www.trafford.com
North America & international
toll-free: 844-688-6899 (USA & Canada)
fax: 812 355 4082

Dedicated with love and affection to
my wife
Marilyn J. Mount,
New Jersey Woman.

Foreword

The black and exact Alaska dawn of an event which greeted Jim Hunter in October, 2003, had one redeeming element. The near-total darkness of it seemed to be mitigated by *dawn's first thin orange line.* A signal of hope that like the long winter nights which crush life in central Alaska, the murder of one friend by another, might somehow end in something more than darkness.

Trapper's Moon is a spellbinding new volume of poems by a man who is becoming one of Alaska's finest poets. The poem telling of the terrible event, **"I Would Write of Red Iris"** yields some of Jim's most striking imagery to date. In fact, his imagery may well have been the only element of the awful events unfolding in the poem which enabled him to preserve his balance.

For along with those images in that particular poem, we also get throughout this book a view of a man who is trying to understand the unyielding dilemmas thrown at him by the essentially hostile universe in which we live. It is a bleak world of cold yet glorious images that produces the murder of one of his trapper friends by another. But in addition to "Iris" this remarkable book gives the reader a broad vision of the poet as philosopher, wilderness dweller, observer of the waste of warfare, grandson of Portuguese immigrants, and environmentalist.

Inspired, as they were in his previous volumes, by long stays in the wilderness of the Alaska Range, Jim's normally terse lines describing loosely based life-changing events come especially home to us through the medium of all those different life-roles.

It must be said, in fact, that Jim's poetry is almost always the product of his own pilgrimage, **his search for meaning on this Earth** of ours that seems forever to be denying him that same meaning. To carry this idea forward another step, we might wish to conclude that all of the various roles through which Jim explores the nature of life are subsets of his major role: **the poet philosopher who can reconcile the terrible violence that characterizes all of life in one minute, and the peaceful coexistence possible the next.**

One minute the lion preys on the lamb and the next minute they lie down together to keep each other warm. Translating that into modern terms, Jim Hunter envisions Alaska as the last outpost of wilderness where man is both hunter, trapper or aggressor and, at the same time, is the wolf's "blue plate special" if the wolf is hungry. Two others of the poems must accompany the reading of "I Would Write of Red Iris." They are "Dressed as a Black Bear Death Came Calling" and "Trapper's Moon."

I would strongly suggest these three poems are a triptych. **"I Would Write of Red Iris"** is filled with those sharp kinds of images which ensure they will never leave our memory. This long poem is essentially the tale of a terrible event. The other two give us the philosopher's metaphoric background against which we can view this heartbreaking occurrence of life's conundrum: the sudden and unexpected upsurge of inexplicable violence.

In **"Dressed as a Black Bear Death Came Calling,"** we have life reduced to a chess game between the poet and a bear – two usually compatible life forms – with some tantalizing added tension resulting from the addition of the philosopher Nietzsche.

The third, **"Trapper's Moon"**, on the other hand, gives us another wild and metaphoric ride through the basic question of life's unpredictability, this time with the utterly beautiful trap set for our destruction by a certain kind of moon that appears only at extremely rare times of the year.

I believe these three poems amount to a brilliant illustration of the basic role of the poet as philosopher. But while Jim Hunter fills this role magnificently in the poems cited and in several others of equal quality, he is also a member of a family, a role represented in this volume by such exquisite and wrenching vignettes as "A White Swan," "Uncle Buddy's Vacant Eyes," "The Woman Who Would Not Swallow," "I Am Going to Go Now," "Raining Love," and "We Watched Like Sparrows."

In fact, every poem in the book deserves a first reading for the narrative and the imagery followed by as many others as may be needed to mine the gold they contain. I would suggest Jim Hunter has given us in *Trapper's Moon* first rights to examine his very soul. The poems should be treated with care, lovingly read – aloud if possible – and then read again another day. Poetry is alive and well in Jim Hunter's gifted hands.

Pierson F. Melcher
Denver, Colorado
September, 2006

Table of Contents

POEMS OF THE WILDERNESS 9

John Haines 10
Dressed As A Black Bear Death Came Calling 11
Logs And Land Patents 14
A Gathering Of Men 15
A Ledge Of Beige Moss....................................... 17
This Summer In These Shadows 19
With Silent Lips Loudly Read 20
So With Us The Planet.. 21
In The Last of Night I Flew 22
The Asylum.. 24
Where Icarus Lived 27
Trapper's Moon 31
Leaving Cabins, Patents, Wildness...................... 34

OF THE FAMILY 35

John Gardner 36
The White Swan 37
Raining Love.. 38
Uncle Buddy's Vacant Eyes 40
The Woman Who Would Not Swallow 50
I Am Going To Go Now....................................... 52
Redemption.. 53
We Portuguese... 54
A Rag Doll Named Judy 60
Casinos 63
Nineteen 64
German She Bear 65
The Toast Whisperer 66
A Five And Dime Of Undone Things 68

The Lady In The Red Coat 72
We Watched Like Sparrows 74
I Went To Bed Young 75
I Would Write Of Red Iris 78

OF WAR 89

Vladimir Mayakovsky 90
The Last Drummer Boy 91
Archimedes 94
White Gravestones Line on Line 95
Galileo, Celeste, and The Patriot Act 97
The Glory, and The Pain 98

OF HUMANITY 104

Francisco Pessoa 105
Dandelions 106
The Maypole Dance 107
A Penguin On The March 108
The Savage Poem Which Rules 109
A Public Dancing Of The Mind 110
A Ladder Of Haiku 111
The Uncaptured Brain 112
In Wilder Fields Still 113
Haiku 114
The Peacock's Truth 116
Idiots 117
Christ In Palm Springs 118
Ballet 119
The Bookcase 120
Before I Was Born 121

POEMS OF THE WILDERNESS

John Haines

pushes his plowshare,
cleaves up the wet and leaning
earth of poems.

Great fertile rows of them
waiting for push sticks
dead salmon and rain.

He makes thoughts
living things
cats' eyes in barbers' mirrors
ice drumming while fog lifts,
gently persistently
like the first sprouts of beans
the wilderness
human climbs out of him.

A fine and a beautiful harvest
lightly scattered
his seeds behave like owl's talons
moonlit or its beak at midnight
as it digs at the rabbit's heart
drags us bloody
from where we are—
to where John is.

12-02-03
Gold King, AK

Dressed As A Black Bear Death Came Calling

In the cabin in night's last hour
as morning came
I lay plagued by Nietzsche
Ecce Homo ethos culture
neither sleeping nor waking
I seemed to find and hold
with the mind's weak hands
a slippery pebble of wild and magic things.
Of how it must have been for him, Nietzsche
so in the darkness I was about to weep
but I am a man, and so did not.

Instead in the excellent silence
in which until that moment I lay still
a creaking of boards rushed me away.

A small bit of my brain
a pinhead of it
an invisible part
hurled me backward.

It was death's slow and certain sound
which shot me away from Nietzsche
threw me back thoroughly to the cave.

I lay a moment stiff and still, a stone half evolved.
For many seconds, I both watched and was.
For as Nietzsche had come to me
so now had death come to my porch
walked the wooden planks of my life
dressed in a black and a heavy step,
clothed me completely in terror too,
death had come to take me away.

So blind is death's determination,
just knowing death was there,
deliberately on my porch
in what was left of the night,
made my hands behind my neck
held yet by the pillow's warmth,
comforted still by the blanket's wool,
go immobile trapped in fear.

So stone still I lay in that last of night
the first of morning, myself wild too,
some kind of wolf
which is how we came
from then to now
when once that was *all* we were,
when once there were more of them than us,
when once we were their prey,
all the way to that morning,
undisturbed in bed with Nietzsche
culture ethos betrayal madness,
until death with a single step,
walked me backward,
sat beside me, sat Nietzsche down too.

Caution worthless I rose
to game with death dressed in black
with Nietzsche too, if he remained?

I am a man, and so I bowed.
I Invited them to debate,
with shotguns, words or chess.
At a round table, or a triangle
their choice, I would not care.
I had risen. I was ready.

I set the pieces
stepped outside
faced them each.

It is the earth then I said
seeing them both
we shall examine
ecce homo culture ethos.

As brothers before the duel we embraced
death dressed as a black bear,
Nietzsche high-collared, I in underwear
each kissed my cheek---invited me then
to a game of chess---I could not win.

So I lay my shotgun down safety off
across my lap, my words my weapons
kissed their cheeks
the man who can not weep
thinking: "Let us see what we shall see?"

I sat willingly then in the last of night
the first of morning,
challenged *them* for their prizes
death dressed as a black bear,
Nietzsche calm smiling philosophic
high collared
me praying,
my second and his second
would seat themselves too
would not fail me—
as I have not you.

09-14-03
Gold King, AK

Logs And Land Patents

The cabin is built of good logs
protects a piece of paper
thumb-tacked to the north wall
typed words to reduce
tangled wilds to straight lines.
A domineering little thing
like my life it lives
below a loaded shotgun
hangs ceremoniously
over coffee cereal beans salt—
keeps the woods barely at bay.

The high ridge pole shares all this regency
big and round it's like a ship's mast
in strong winds it twists and creaks,
in the worst storms it heaves upward
as if it too is frightened
for it groans out loud painfully
an increasingly desperate ship
my life similarly
all these great heaving's
mark it down, make me God fearing.

On calm days here it's a green Eden
wide valleys of motionless trees
gray slabs of ridges running fat to the south
beyond them bold peaks sharp with white snow.

The land patent and I observe it all
a quiet and a defiant pair—
we slave toward definition.

07-09-04
Gold King, AK

14

A Gathering Of Men

Last night we formed a circle
as powerless as September leaves,
settled like them into our places.

Last night we were volcanoes
living here where we do
long dormant, not yet dead.

Last night a second gravity grew,
something molten to be obeyed
for at three that very morning
like an omen Mars had come
not a seeming star but something real
to be separately defined:
"That is not a star. That is Mars."

Mars separate and whole
looked like a second moon
a tiny one but there
as we were last night
men before the hunt
imitation moons of mammoth hunters
something good
and whole about it
story telling,
male laughter.

Last night while it was dark
by firelight we made a plan
an important one
with prodding and with pride
a little war dance before the fact
"First rule: One shot and all gather,"
Someone said.

And knowing the rules
were none of them last night made
but were with reverence
in some way hypnotic
repeated
as had Mars in its orbit
repeated
so had we ours—
of the hunt.

09-13-03
Gold King, AK

A Ledge Of Beige Moss

I found a ledge of beige moss
pale with green lichens
laid myself down to sleep.

Wondered briefly
while I slept
if caribou
would nibble my hair
spring griz,
dangerous with hunger,
might kill me
gorge on my bones and on my blood,
as had I on others?

I was as far as I could go—
twenty-six miles from the cabin
it was some time near noon
but I was no nearer the sun.

So I chose to sleep
and peacefully slept.

I was a traveler that day from another time
un-tethered, standing still,
dreams intact, forever in flight—

I woke an hour later
surrounded by snow still and hard
sunburned and warm,
came awake on hope's highest cliffs.

I was an hour older,
and my wings had melted
so soundly had I slept.
I knew not when waking
on what planet I might be
in this wilderness or that
or much cared.

So I lay more then on beige moss
neither asleep nor awake
until I shook my head
and saw everything there about me
all again.

I had not died,
but I *was* in some paradise,
even awake,
high there on that highest plateau
canyons all about
all alone alive and well,
all and each of us
in that house of those gods
we'd had one more hour—
one at least.

04-08-03
Wood River, AK

This Summer In These Shadows

There live the tallest trees
where shafts of light
slide downward secretly and full,
to the lowest moss
of the forest I am.

I stand outlined, human
not one animal seen
but one who watches
my step and my walk
this summer in these shadows
that animal moves nearby
through the fragile ferns
which spread
like hands with palms out
as I come to a place
where unmistakably
wolf paws have ripped the soil
politely covered scat
differently
than wolves teeth at the killing
which are savage
my neck tilts to study it
the complicated forest of my brain
which like me
El Lobo almost knows
(through this summer and in these shadows
in which we live)
why.

12-08-03
Fairbanks, AK

With Silent Lips Loudly Read

On all sides wilderness
mountain walls in all directions
halfway to the sky
layered and gray
snow sifted and purple
piled and open
they held a library of events
stony and still.

Shouting without moving
great gray sphinxes
four quadrants in code
I sat then in their cradle
in among the clouds high up myself
trapped on the earth
looking down at it all
on that day
small
alone
invisible
a dot
with a smaller dot
we call a brain
viewing all those layers
of all that's been
which I had reached
with silent lips loudly read.

01-23-04
Gold King, AK

So With Us The Planet

Water carries brown earth,
like busy ants to its certain doom.

Water works
deeper and deeper
until cunning as a sunrise
lies a canyon—
unexpected
and yet not—

so with the wind
so the mountains—

so with the sea
so the sea shore—

so with us
so the planet.

09-11-03
Gold King, AK

In The Last of Night I Flew

I lay alone in the mountains
with light falling like water
when I began to wake.
I heard the clipped sounds
it seemed of children at play?

(I shall have to rise I thought
to see *who* they are,
and *what* they are doing?)

Or was it already day?
Or sometime in between
when I heard them?

It had been very faint
that laughing and calling
but clearly it *was* children,
chattering or in some debate?

So I came more awake
for there was something in them
too of omen or of alarm
a strange tablet of sound from somewhere
or a dream of a headstone laying flat,
a morning hieroglyph to be deciphered?

Then it hit me
in the half exactness of where I woke
where uninvited things arrive
misfit thoughts leap on stage
actors with lines, but not with names.

It was geese or sand hill cranes
calling and calling
up high, hard to see
our children or us theirs
flying where we can not
as whales and others
swim where we can not
each with eerie sounds all the way
children
too simple we know
to comprehend.

So I wondered rising from my bed
hearing them searching for south
right above where I'd just slept
as if they were confused
as to which way was theirs
which way was mine
children seeking something.

So shoeless out I went
stood barefoot looking up
I tell you I did
myself in that purest of mornings
alive and innocent
so in that first of dawn
or last of night I flew —
I joined them
circled high up there with them
in their confusion
or not.

08-30-03
Gold King, AK

The Asylum

First a fierce storm, then the trees breathe quietly
for the wildness of it had been frightening
turned the day to something harsh
fear filled the clouds with spite
sound arrived from somewhere else
even in the gray of it
colors went wildly radiant—
deadly even—
in April as the mountains forgave me.

A peculiar sullenness it was afterward
then a complete and raging brightness
from the mountain's top
and my senses one by one abandoned me
went off to live alone with the great peaks
perpetually white
and down below to the forest ferns
and to places with planes and angles
always before in another form seen.

The after-storm silence left me senseless,
changed the asylum halted its usual rule,
made me question
how long before we came
chained as the earth is to the sun,
how long had each of them
without us so perfectly spun?

How long had this place
then—
with its own noises only,
its *own* sounds,
like those I was now not hearing
waited for us
not to discover it,
but to discover itself without us?

I saw in the after-storm
a math of hope,
the Mayan zero of what is,
flawless sacred and pure—
I watched silence kiss space
colorful and complete empty of us,

I was nailed to the formula,
and I became on the high peak
a deep earth diver,
as the binding of my molecules
skipped beats
rearranged themselves
closed my eyes for me
opened my mind
made me nearly free
made me deaf, deaf at last
on top the mountain stunned and still
I stood free
outside the fence of senses
thank god and glad

such a mountain or meadow still exists
proof we've not yet
burned the craft on which we thrive
from port to port
in ceaseless circles—
consuming fiendishly.

I was forced up there sitting
to wonder what keeps us
every day from knowing—
then knew.

So I left and down I went
booted and hard
back to the asylum—
the one in which we live
back down the mountain
obeying gravity a fly to the spider's web
back willingly to the ill cacophony.

Back to where down the mountain
facts and senses once more
tied my tongue and strapped me down—
like each and all of us willingly to prison
babes in the asylum cradle-bound
spider's silk on me did wrap-around.

04-08-03
Gold King, AK

Where Icarus Lived

Like a blinded moth I'd flown
branded too to the highest snows
slopes like angels deep with joy
carried me upward easily borne.

Only by looking back
could I grip how high I'd come
how the snow had burned me
how sharply all around the cliffs fell.

How quickly from there I could fall
be Icarus dead again in animal tracks
moss snow and rocks my only path,
a tightrope to a last and final ledge
until far past the noon of my life
I sat a great overlook
looked down to a separate paradise
frozen lakes and wolves dens a worthy sight.

I could see
high there from my dangling rope
my negotiated day
all the way south
in my imagination
clear to Anchorage even.

I could see to the north
what of my life was left
all there was to see:
Wolverine Mountain
the sky to the earth
and on to Fairbanks
and beyond there even to the Whites
and clear thought.

Not one cloud
for the fifth day straight
cluttered this place
over paradise
or anything anywhere else.

Each knoll had its own red sentry
fox tracks at port arms
as my life and I passed
one one-way one the other
on our way to where we were.

It was yesterday I'd flown
too close to the sun
sat there on top at last
to shade my eyes,
even my mind.

For the view was hypnotic
serious and still
it tried to pull me down
to fly me to the river below
to where my mind would swim

where it and where I
would all together run
all north and all south
hemmed in on all sides
by the gray and the purple
by the black and massive walls of rock
but me dangerous and sane
I stayed riveted to the top.

I stood then
in that Godly house
where like they
in every direction I could see
little moth or not
compulsion satisfied.

For straight above me
straight up higher yet
high in the highest blue
another ballet began
where other sons flew
spun ungodly figure eights
left thin trails of white.

I welcomed them
irreverent with their kerosene
into this place, ours both
I on the earth
them in the sky
crossing final ridges
each blindly to his own beast.
Of wings and of horses
ownership alone
meant nothing that day.

All depended
on other things mysterious
but certain and sure
where Icarus dared fly.

On good luck,
the will of Zeus,
old testimony or new.

On skill on experience
on a desperate need to be
where no others are
not only to embrace it
but equally so
to wed it—
where Icarus lives
but leave me not here
read on instead if you dare..

04-12-03
Wood River, AK

Trapper's Moon

I

It was the tracks gave it away
seized the trappers' mind,
wolverine tracks trapper's gold.

I'd seen it gleaming once before
hope's bright stone
alive in another's eye now long dead
that tone of reverence
of moons and wolverines,
not boldly as with wolves
lynx marten, other fur.

No.
In this trappers' voice and in the other's
it was there clearly to see
a northern reverence
sure and pure:
"Saw wolverine tracks today.
Over on Last Chance creek."
Conjures up tenacity fierceness cunning
hats of value long white fangs, bared.
The driving off of wolves of bears
even of moons.

No one in his right mind
fools with moons or wolverines.
Enters such wild space absent fear
Places their footprint solidly down
something ancient, few will ever do.

II

So over the mountain the trapper came
the last of dark the first of day
to seek the tracks, see them, study them
find their mark, measure their weakness
a professor of what to do
spread apart the jaws of steel
lightest step snaps them shut.
There was out there too
an odd and a circling moon gone mad
desperately still, a wolverine itself
huge, silent, dangerous in the sky
the moon the wolverine which is which
both wild in the Alaska night
roaming fierce and free
one in the sky one in the earth
daring us to be with them.
The moon makes of night day
the moon lights the wolverine's eye
Then the moon the wolverine the trapper
become one great knot, an earthly constellation.

III

The moon too had left its track
night and day, it never set
crept morning noon and night
yellow in the one, white in he other
like a white wolverine it left a track
behind the mountains it secretly went
stealthy too between great spruce
lit the wolverine's tracks
lit the wolverine's eye.

IV

So as the distant ridge is topped
where final important signals live
battle between animal and man begins
always has always will
where the trap will be set
where steel jaws will snap
where elusive creatures
shall at last be caught
the moon then
from behind the mountain suddenly appears
Grendel round and golden almost beige
Latin seas of sand and brown
tales to tell above the ridge it leaps
defines with shadows the wolverine's track
no fleeing comet this wild moon
steadfast adversary instead
glowering glowing and whole
might swallow itself anything wild
man or wolverine
display or dream
for any who see it that way
it is a great and a fearsome thing
in the morning out from hiding
the trapper's camera quickly snaps
traps the moon for what it is.

Gold King, Alaska
January 16th, 2006
(For Ron..)

33

Leaving Cabins, Patents, Wildness

Leaving the cabin I ride the sky
truth from the ground up into the air
before me changes masks
I see a necklace of white rocks—

Objects once large quickly shrink
white rocks become a delicate necklace
trees tall and slender its throat
the forest a lawn on which to lay.

The cord which fed me
kept me tied to the earth
held me prisoner—
is cut, release is sweet.

Flight does it
teaches me anew chords I rarely heard
ruins facts again and solid hypotheses
the hypnosis of the single sense
of the many is destroyed—

Flight insists I accept instead
not just white rocks now in fact tiny,
(Illegitimate even)
but all else beyond them.

All else I might ever feel see or be
for is not everything
flight insists I wager—
illusory?

07-22-04
Fairbanks, AK

OF THE FAMILY

John Gardner

Born in 33
dead by the Shenandoah
by Harley in 82
if nothing else
sensed an essential
in the American Riot
before his death at 49
of all we might be
at our best
potential realized
or not.

A Roman who never drank lead
killed instead by culture
tamed Grendel but not gravity
saw the lines of what is
intersect with the saying of it
breathed in sight
made words a telescope
the Milky Way of human wonder
wandered out there
launched unruly rafts of thought
on a stormy finding sea—
he balanced ambivalence.

02-22-04
Gold King, AK

The White Swan

It was a cold January in 42.
I leaned forward from the back seat
when I was four-and-a-half
in our small car, a 39 Dodge coupe
my little brother still moist hours old
swaddled in white in the front seat
cradled between mother and father
a furious and a precious moment
like a child's top it spun my brain
a gift a gift the cerebellum cried!
like a separate force
before my eyes lay the babe a special thing—

Trailing delicious joy together we ran
mother and I into the five-and-dime
father double-parked on Main.

The toy counter was high above
but there lay the whitest of white swans
from somewhere graceful pure and perfect it had come
for my new little brother plastic necked, it would float
a grand feeling exiting Woolworth's on the run
back to our Dodge where on the seat
as the baby watched
I presented him wrapped
that whitest of white swans
to be with him in all his baths to come
and in a royal way—
gone before I knew him fully
dead in 88 from an overdose.

08-04-04
Fairbanks, AK

Raining Love

My little brother
found as usual his certain corner
of our big living room
where gray rectangles of sunlight
filtered in the front windows
of our west-facing house
lit lazy and rising bits of dust.

He curled himself there against the hardwood
below the window and sunlit debris
big-eyed as usual.
My mother was defiant,
but not a caged tigress either,
uncaged stalking
neutral snarling.

My father seemed like a lion tamer
Armed not with a whip, but with paper
for it was dollar bills he hurled at her
and they seemed to float upwards
not down (Which was strange)
and then to fall from the ceiling
like rain in slow motion
like a French movie.
I can see them still
from where I stood
the dollar bills green and wrinkled
some wadded into balls
the better to war with.

I can still hear my father's moan and shout
his hoarse voice with its afternoon edge
slightly raspy with bits of whiskey,
"What do you mean I don't love them?"

I hear clearly even today each word:
"Do you see that roof?"
I see clearly even today his single finger
pointed directly to the ceiling
down from which floated the dollar bills
and then like a lawyer
the next interrogative
"Do you see food on that table?"

For there in the dinning room
sat dinner half-finished
from which we had all just fled
my mother brandishing
absent any fear whatsoever
tightly gripped with both hands
as if it were a baseball bat
the black wrought-iron
of the fireplace poker
with which to strike my father.
"That is love!", he explained.

And so in Stockton we came that spring again
my brother at 4 in his corner
crouching and half-hidden
beneath those shafts of magical light
and me at 9 between them all
in April—
to learn what love was.

02-03-04
Fairbanks, AK

Uncle Buddy's Vacant Eyes

Uncle Buddy's umbilical to this earth
was cut for good in mid-42
where shipped to Guadalcanal
he met other young men
Japanese who like him
spoke bayonet.

"Guadalcanal"
a word for our protection
the family whispered
at five I digested its infamy
and a half-century later
the whole war's haunting
has had its effect

Uncle Buddy
who was really
my much older first cousin
had an exact age beyond mine
for some reason
kept a mystery.

When he returned from the war
I was 9
able as a child
to identify something
correctly forever.

What I saw was hidden there
Deeply and dark in his Portuguese eyes
a deep brown and mute thing
black boots and sea weed
cork perhaps
or machine guns gone deaf too
which at night in his dreams
could still be heard
through his smile I felt him
second generation American
my mother's brother's son
a Bettencourt
at 22 already absent.

His father married thirteen times
we remain untamed
American Gypsies
among us
Uncle Harold
a navigator of women,
Uncle Buddy's Dad.

My guess is Uncle Buddy
at 13 years older than me
my first cousin
made him in 41
17 and drafted
to Guadalcanal
boys killing other boys
for older men
he fought
from wet trenches and dry trees
watched his own blood
on dead brown earth pool
mix with the earth with ease.

Bodies by bodies lay
uniforms by uniforms
shoulder to shoulder
in trenches and out that decisive month
August 42
filled not just with water
but every sort of human scream,
the special scents of death,
the incessant hum of flying lead
all the time, but especially at night.

So it was then the artist began.
He cut a message
on top Uncle Buddy's pupils
that landscape of screams
to the perceptive whispering
in particular to children
don't even knock,
no one is home.

A scrimshaw on his eyes not of Moby Dick,
of harpoons or of ivory,
rather of other agonies,
the architecture of war,
silent and hysterical carvings
spelling to me at 9
in an ancient language
I somehow already knew,
say nothing.
No one will answer.
No one is there.

II

In Tracy, California
we were in the front yard
watering at 100 degrees
gently my summer at 12
when Uncle Buddy remarked
of Guadalcanal
his underwear had rotted off
as others around him, jerked,
ruptured by lead and by steel,
bleeding as they ate bleeding as they slept,
in the trenches
out of the trenches
young men from here
directed to do so
killed young men from there,
using long knives and short swords
puncturing in time honored ways
in daylight and in moonlight
abdomens and ribs and hearts,
all the while bowing and cursing
and no one
even thinking
not even me,
for I yearned for it,
in my own certain kind of child's madness
of killing war instead.

On Guadalcanal Uncle Buddy woke to death
went to sleep with death
slept fitfully in the arms of death
woke wet for weeks on end
if not from water from sweat.

He watched young lieutenants
come and go
and corporals and sergeants he replaced.
He came home with three stripes
burned diagonally
across his cerebellum
belli causi medivici
and burned outside too
across his smiling brown eyes.

Smiling, I at 12 assumed,
at the angels he had seen,
inside the house of madness,
in which he'd been marooned.

Much later he denied
telling me anything
and never told me more.
And in fact it was,
when he had spoken of it at all
as if I were not there,
for although he was looking at me,
it was to the sky he seemed to speak,
as only one spot of lawn,
received any watering.

For having in his own eyes
I now believe
for having ever spoken at all,
meant he'd betrayed something,
to which he'd made a vow,
in his sleep perhaps,
or while his eyes
were being carved,
his brain etched

with war,
about which
he must have sworn
on return
to never speak.

And only that once did
other than his life,
of course.

III

When I was 14
and he by the calendar 27,
my blessed Uncle Buddy
let me ride his motor scooter,
always smiled,
never angry,
looked around with those eyes,
and married,
and told anyone who cared
in 51 who would listen,
all he wanted was a job,
a place to work,
a home to come home to,
a yard to care for,
normalcy,
and never never,
war anymore.

IV

Across the street in Fairbanks
here 50 years later now
I see this man today
just a bit older than I
limping now
who might be uncle Buddy
but is not.
At 17 he went to war
not to Guadalcanal in 42
but to Korea in 51
packing a radio
to Chosen Reservoir
came home
said the same.

I was born in a magic circle
a date called 37,
so I was sent to neither place,
although at 17 myself
like a bee to pollen
I joined the Cold War,
humans entwined again
like great summons
circling the earth
shouting loudly kill.

But it was somber men
who in my child's brain
and in my life had lain
who by their presence,
made of me somber too.

Their eyes told me of it,
their hearts were absent parts
I could see
were more like clocks
wound by strangers,
ribs no longer bone
a new metal blocking hope,
and other things from getting in,
other than gardening,
and a desire to never never
do it again.

V

It has been a long time
since I flew to California
at Uncle Buddy's behest,
who himself gave me my choices:
"Carry my coffin,
or chat my bed."

I chose myself by then at 56 the bedside chat
as between white sheets,
and his sucking of cigarettes,
I watched him die,
not at Guadalcanal,
though most of him there had,
but rather in Tracy smiling still,
from cigarettes
pure and simple.

I think we must ask
what it is with war
what part of each other
besides our bodies we kill?

Rome poisoned itself with lead.
We do it with war and with plenty.
We grow fat in body
not lean in mind,
so that with the two:
the curse of plenty
and the sword of war
we have driven that sword
into our own belly
kneeling we commit hara-kiri
finally ourselves Japanese
accidentally.

I think we Americans
must ask ourselves
how we dare,
make of the man across my street
and of Uncle Buddy too,
and in some ways myself,
war's children,
hollow eyed, garden bound,
if not in bondage,
amputees still,
meant to leap hedges,
but never will.

VI

I see it coming.
A time when
war itself
like a fire
burning backwards
will turn itself upside down.

For if lead pipes
killed Rome
and too much plenty is killing us
beware more of war,
which shall kill everything
forever,
kill even uncle Buddy's
vacant eyes,
kill even
the hushed,
slippered steps,
of my neighbor's life.

07-02-03
Fairbanks, AK

The Woman Who Would Not Swallow

We went to visit
saw a friend's mother
who like mine was dying,
slowly with Alzheimer's
they said.

"I am here mother."
he said. "This is my friend."

She took my hand
looked deeply once into my eyes
her mouth pursed
a taut line, definite
relaxed, determined.

Her legs were like a doll's
straight out and rigid at eighty-eight
her face perfectly made-up
with eyes which saw us
we think, in Escondido
she seemed a mime
the place so nice,
ownership and help
pure Mexican
she never budged.

"If we are going to talk," my friend pleaded.
"you must swallow."
They have given her a cracker,
he told me.
She refuses to swallow it.
Which I had already observed.

We stayed for his kisses and his coaxing
but though her eyes saw us
and she'd accepted my hand,
like death mimed,
she never spoke,
nor my eyes ever again met.

My friend and I left on a path
of concrete.
He turned leaving and said to her,
the woman who would not swallow:
"Mother. If you wish to speak to me,
you must swallow."
She did not.

On the way home
through thin, winding streets
between small, brown, hot hills,
we left her there
the woman stone still
refusing absolutely to swallow
so Lorca then
to the son spoke
fuente claro
rio serene.

It is all she has,
Lorca said to him
Let her have it.

09-27-03
Escondido, CA

I Am Going To Go Now.

In September she refused to swallow
In January she went
seated, looking off somewhere
you could see
drugged
of course
ravaged
of course
made up
dressed well
patrician
royal even
waiting patiently for a dignitary
other than us
to pay her a visit
like a queen
she sat very still
viewing the brown hills of her kingdom
from a porch of ours
a straight-backed chair
until when water came
she dismissed it, and all it meant,
stiff-wristed refused it,
pronounced her last ultimatum
"No, thank you. I am going to go now,"
she said.

And did.

01-31-04
Fairbanks, AK

Redemption

You the teacher
once young to the classroom
then each year a year older
and they
them always the same
blending
until your departure.

Some younger teacher arrives,
arrives with equal hope,
to teach
you to pasture unredeemed
coupons unsent—
until one day
to you,
you with a cane
come some few
waylay you with praise
for those invisible things
you did
not for yourself
for them—
they redeem you.

06-15-04
Fairbanks, AK

We Portuguese

My mother took me aside
before I knew
something was wrong—
It was a seriousness
something you know—
she had been arrested
she explained
in 1947 when I was 10
she had been a fool
so I would not be
blindsided at school that day
she would not do it again
and she did not,
We Portuguese.

She wore pants and sweatshirts.
The next year, 1948
she called my brother and I to her
and said "Jimmy, Dennis. Listen to me.
I am going to tell you something."

I figured someone had died
I knew
and someone did.

She explained we were Portuguese
to my little brother and I.
we would be teased
at school
asked "Which geese did not fly?"
If our father's were black?
If our cousin was "Manual Labor?"

The serious teaching of it—
an endless sea of mothers
and their milk—
an endless chain of children
still it was a shock to learn
we two little boys
though our name was Hunter
we were Portuguese.

We ate linquisa
milked cows
grew alfalfa
married Afonsos
kin of kings
grew cork
stood not at Gibraltar,
with the British or any others,
but with gypsies in wide skirts
colorful which rustled
attacked Castle Carcassone
and anything else in view—
further and further out still
alone if need be
forever navigating
We Portuguese.

We changed our names
to be British or Spanish.
Anything to have a ship
a poem
a bird to set free
an ocean to swallow us,
We Portuguese.

Pessoa said
born in 1888
what matters
is knowing how to see
(13 March 1914)
and so we have seen
We Portuguese

Magellan Magalhao
said in 1520
he would sail around the world
and did,
dying on the way, Portuguese

The Pope said
Spain shall have
this half the earth
Portugal the other
which left us,
We Portuguese,
with Japan
which properly
they resented
those Japanese.

God left us with Macao,
we searchers
so we sought instead
what there is to know.

The first man on the moon
northern European
American.

The first man to the stars
where we have already been
will be Portuguese.
which have shown the way before,
and shall show it yet again.

Our little swath of brown earth,
mountains, old cliffs by the sea,
villages of white walls, red roofs
our Sebastian myth,
our tiny foothold on earth
keeps Spain, all else at bay
our islands stretch far and far away.

Watch our sailor's minds
made of sea swells
mermaid hips
the slap of oars
the last great ocean
the silence of space.

We taste the lilt and the roar of Lorca
our Spanish friend in dreams,
We Portuguese.

Lorca would dance with us
praise extremely wild magic
all colored orbs undiscovered
paint for us and us for him
black sunrises red oceans
white skies of dainty lace.

We look past earth
beyond Hell's shore Heaven's hem
to a final and future time
where once again we all shall be—
We Portuguese.

Our minds are set
not just to the sextant
but also too to its stars
to the whale's song
the mermaid's emerald hair
to the most ignored stomach
in the rockiest land
of the thinnest goat.

We know at birth
we Portuguese
the precise steps to dances
not yet invented.
quem passar o Cabo de nam
ou tornara ou nam*
we know at birth.

When know before our eyes open
our graves in a nameless place wait.
We know defeat, and victory too.

We would rather
pick a man up
than strike him down.

Call him friend
if he would let us,
enemy should he choose.

Clear fountains clearly heard
serene rivers observed.

We have seen much
from Portugal—
from this round port too
to convince us—
we shall be going
shall be leaving again
as always before we have.

Should gravity
block our way
patiently like water
we shall watch and we shall wait
and strongly still
unbowed
will leave anyway
with it or without it
gravity's choice
we care not
We Portuguese.

09-21-03
Gold King, AK

*

  "He who passes Cape Not
   may return or may not."

Fifteenth Century Portuguese sailor's saying. Until then few
dared sail ships down Africa's coast beyond current day
Morocco, which is where Cabo Nam then existed, not far from
today's Canary Islands. It was thought beyond that point the sea
boiled, and the earth ended. Hard to believe, but true. Today's
parallel Cabo Nam or "boiling sea" is of course gravity.

A Rag Doll Named Judy

My mother died when I was born.

My half-sister was eight
half-brother eleven
it was hard
grandma took us in —
She loved us.
I called her mama.

She raised us
in Los Angeles in the heat
I was a little girl
jeaned and bare foot.

My father married a lady named Nora.
When grandma died I was sent to them.

My brother and sister
went to other relatives
my brother ran away
much later married —
sis made it back to L.A., San Pedro,
got through high school
lived with an aunt
helped with her kids
(That Aunt passed away just a week ago
can you imagine —
my last blood relative from then.)

Dad and Nora sent a lawyer
down from Seattle to San Pedro
to bring me up here.

Lawyer wore a gray suit
a fedora hat.
My sister stayed home from school
that day I wondered why
it was to say good-bye
she knew I was going
I did not.

I stayed with the lawyer that night
and my rag doll named Judy
with big eyes,
and a blue and white checked outfit.

Judy had very rosy cheeks
yellow hair made from yarn
no suitcase no clothes
Judy and I on December 7th 1946
arrived at Boeing Field.
Many arms
reached down for me —
all at one time.

Today I am sixty-four years old
saw my brother and sister
maybe two times
I was lucky
having someone who took me.

Today I can see the white blouse
under the blue overalls I wore
1n 1946 California sandals
never owned a dress in my life
before Maple Valley, Washington
three strangers
four, including my father—
met me at the airport
took me in.

The first night I thought
grasping Judy tightly
if I could just get to sleep real fast
I would wake up at home again
safe
just Judy and I
Oh God I was scared.

Each time my children turn seven
now theirs' turning seven
I worry you know.

How would they adapt
if someone took them away
to live with strangers
abruptly in a strange place
without siblings
anyone they trusted?

I've gone on too long—
perhaps.

05-24-04
Maple Valley, WA
For Cuz 1

Casinos

In San Diego we were spent
we fled the machines
reassured ourselves
outside in bright sun
we were winners.

We smelled cactus
red appled and thorny
heard car locks snap upward
felt chrome handles cooked
baked by the sun
stood on pavement and worked hard
to measure money
against what is important
uncertain on full stomachs
gamblers and seekers
miners too of knowing.

In the hellish heat
we prospected for reason
even while praying secretly
for jackpots,
for sweet release from gravity
hell better yet from the body,
told ourselves money had never ruled us,
money measured nothing
in the desert there—
we totaled up our winnings.

09-30-03
Escondido, CA

Nineteen

It seems now
as if we had always been
as if all the other
never was
was preparation for now
as if we had arrived
as if this place was always ours
special and complete
our Cinderella with no midnight
as you are here for me
I am here for you
and now we have nineteen
and nineteen to go
for thirty-eight
I'll see you there—
don't be late.

I love you.

06-14-04
Fairbanks, AK

German She Bear

Images flash by
of women in armor
with swords
but something else
about them
not to do with either
differentiates
more powerfully perhaps
whatever
it is good to have one by my side
remembering the time the cyclist
and I were at it
and the she bear rushed out
now another parking lot fight
tire-chains and jack-handles
this time against another enemy
arrives this strange non-male
cloud-splitting lightning bolt
attached to heaven I imagine
certainly not earth
my German she bear
I welcome her
with a smile.

03-04-04
Fairbanks, AK

The Toast Whisperer

Born in Denver in 45
Fairbanks, Alaska in 70
hard to miss.

Twenty-five years young
youthful, dynamic.
full of life of hope
of energy, of strength.

We were sitting with her
unchanged
after all life had thrown at her
60 years young
on her final day full of life
of hope,
of energy
of strength.

She taught Kindergarten
so much else too.
Taught the other "K" kindness
good behavior, love, determination.

The night she left us
she was still buttering our toast
a toast whisperer
(Listen!)
morning noon and night.
Neither to horses nor ghosts
the human spirit
Barbara whispered
through her own rich self.

Coffee came sugared
herself in kindness
toast came buttered whispering boldly
"As I am kind to you,
so may you be kind to others.

II

Wife, mother, teacher, friend, advisor
toast whisperer.

Each and all of us
knew her
her kindnesses
and now know
more than ever
in her passing
what we have lost.

We honor her best
by finding then
in our own way
as she did
every day
feet to wash
toast to butter—
our own whispering messages
the ones she taught
to send--

11-23-05
Fairbanks, AK
For Barbara Lang.

A Five And Dime Of Undone Things

Since packing the last of it
a year has passed
three since she died.

The carefully labeled boxes
"Mother's Desk packed 5/02"
and
"Mother's Framed Photos packed 6/01"
and,
you get the picture.

She chose 29 February to go
first year of the new century
and that day I thought
holding her hand as she died
reading Timothy,
because a nurse had called me back,
"Good for you, mother!"
"Go Woman, Go!"

Now I deal with cardboard boxes
the ashes of her life
left in my lap
the sole surviving son
and I tell myself
many before have done this
in fact everyone
so why is it then,
so incredibly hard?

First I felt resentment
loss
knowing I was next,
that she was not easy to love,
impossible to understand.

Now the final feeling
is none of those,
rather an assortment of awful regret,
a five and dime of undone things,
time and trinkets unbestowed,
now never to be,
for as King of my time,
I behaved badly.

Simple appreciation of age
I might have shared
but did not.
And much else
as the strong son, I never did
for I was a man and that was all.

So now I do the boxes
the safety pins
the spools of thread
the needle with thread still in it
in a plastic box
with cotton on the bottom.

And her in-your-face pins
"The Immoral Majority"
and "Senior Power"
and "Gray Panthers"
and
you get the picture.

Box after box
trying to sort it all out
unable.
What do you throw away?
What do you keep?

Is her spirit watching me
or not?
Is there even a spirit?

Losing a mother is a terrible thing,
something we all do,
and go through the mess of it:
her hair brush with hair in it,
candles half-burnt,
broken pieces of things
to one day be fixed.
Cigarette ashes.

A little brass donkey,
pulling a little brass cart.
My God!
What am I to *do* with it?

I touch all those things
trigger a lifetime of images
of my brother and I young,
of her rebellious in slacks,
of her five feet of full
one-hundred-percent
Portuguese woman power,
of my poor father,
of the poor world,
neither a match,
for the things she did.

All to end up here
in Fairbanks, Alaska
on Two-South
dying
with such fine women
circled around her
tough as nails
nurses dressed in white
like her
now the boxes
of her all there is.

No great ceremony
here in America
only the black
sorting out,
of it.

08-24-03
Fairbanks, AK

The Lady In The Red Coat

A light rain, though not cruel greets us
the streets are heavy with yellow leaves.

But in the half-darkness fall gives mornings
there is in this rain more than a usual sadness.

Out my window and down the street
there is a lady walking slowly and alone
somehow herself a season slowly ending
something on which might be a raincoat
but in my eye seems more a woman's old robe
bright red, soft, damp, fluffy
itself in all the yellow and gray and dampness
around it autumn's brightest red leaf.
I watch her through Venetian blinds
below her robe see her old white socks
collapsed around bare ankles
is she cold?

With sidewalks so near
why walk in the street?

Her head is down slightly, but she is determined
and her walk, though not yet a shuffle
will soon enough be one.

This particular morning
of her life, and of mine
she and her coat become
all the brightness we each have
briefly though the window glass.

I see it then
out the peep-hole of my own beliefs
through the thick and foggy mist of her loneliness
which clings to her as much as the old robe itself
shifting before me as she moves slowly closer
I feel her aches, and her ancient stubbornness
that red and proud glory of long suffering women
which seems to blossom fully
in old women totally alone
for once in the past—
we had spoken.

09-23-04
Fairbanks, AK

We Watched Like Sparrows

Before February
everything was indefinite
surely life would end—
but not soon.

One morning the drapes were pulled,
and there on the lawn cancer stood,
turned life's hourglass;
the whole world in fact—
upside down.

Day and night the sand spoke cruelly,
whispered its hissing little truth,
like wasted blood, flowed through
hope's glass waist so tiny and precise.

We watched like sparrows
as gravity in February
like a thief used our sand, then—
delivered something unexpected,
chained to cancer it came—
better behavior its name.

03-04-04
Fairbanks, AK

I Went To Bed Young

I went to bed young
woke old.
Only a day earlier
I'd worn boldly
with youthful turbulence
a maroon shirt of good wool
thick and warm
below it a cotton shirt
the lightest of lilac purple
a fine and dancing mixture
a declaration of races run
but woke with hands I could not curl
nor fists longer make.

I've gone to dangerous places
rarely conflict refused,
but this day I woke a captive
a night time coup
left pain enthroned
my grandfather's fingers were mine now
(I can see him pointing to them
his words and smile wrapped
in pleasant resignation.)
and hear plainly his phrase
"They will not close."

I went to sleep
with a fist I could make,
woke today
trapped in a universe of fists

with fingers unfit to slap.
Once I walked
a kind of leader
not looking back
for leaders must always see
what might lie ahead
but today I woke
with only backs to see.

The very testes
of my fingers curl
in an ignorant and ignominious way
little signals they are
the outposts of my body
checking in and checking out
a code of rot and of decay
like old trees which give fire,
at night make you warm
I too like them now must fall
feeding the earth and helping us all.

Yesterday I went to bed a youth
today I wake an old man
hauling about no longer invisible
exactly who I am.

I would hide it from time to time
from mirrors and others about
from all who would see me
and too from gravity
if only there were a way.

I would chase it away
with push-ups and weights
mountains and rivers
with crystal mines and planes
with love
with fearless joy
with the drunkenness of youth
if I had not gone to bed young
only to wake old.

If the cruel trick
I knew was coming
had just not come
if birth's great gift
had not
like the universe itself
quietly exhausted
secretly when I was not looking—
I would still be young.

But even though
I went to bed a young man
and woke the way I have
I have fooled them still
and my grandfather too
for I with my own tricks
slept always secretly old.

So this morning I dress with it
and shamble simply along
wearing my grandfather's little grin—
as blessed I am—
just to wake again.

03-21-04
Gold King, AK

I Would Write Of Red Iris

I would write of red iris
of things exquisite
if I were able
of how women
of Chinese royalty walk
of white birds gliding to a blue river
of pink alpenglow off lazy clouds
of lines straight and true
a telegraph of joy
if two men were not dead
and a third, a dead man walking.

I would write of red iris
if they existed
of things exquisite in their beauty
if death on willow street
riding an innocent horse
had not like raven landed there
glided downward from the left
ate of the old and rotting kill
had not lit that morning so recent
painted with bullets and blood
if the closing circle had not clicked shut
if Mike himself while being shot
had not made of two others guilty or not
dead men dead
in Fairbanks that morning
now noon never to know.

I

It was in a cloudy place
by any description
and by all the powers that be
that I met the first in the forest
and in the city later
lost them both.

We had never met before
first Ron and I
nor to each other would we ever lie
when first I heard of him then next saw
almost cherubic he was
Oklahoma claimed
Californian born
who like a brother
one of the wilderness
I learned to love
for loving the wilderness
is a lonely and a terrible thing
no worse mistress worries men
we each at times to the other would admit.
I will not express here
those thousand moments which bound us
would write of other beauties
of red iris if I were able.

I would write of dawn's
first thin orange line
of that day's promise
not of light
perhaps
if not of heat
of blue sky hopefully

if only an hour of it
of some glorious sun
if only an hour of it,
if not death on Willow Street
and its ruined hour had not come.

II

Another man came to the mountain valley
blue-eyed and tall
a mixture of myth and bears
of mountain sheep and caribou
a child's smile
delirious nearly
too with the love of it
the eyes were straight and true
then we were three.

He came down the slopes
of life
a purposeful stride
I would write of the beauty
he saw
he felt
if I were able.
I would not write
what went wrong
in Alaska
in the mountains and in the valleys
along that creek named by death
where two men
and I the third climbed.

It was nearing ten years
when something at Buzzard Creek
went terribly wrong
when two men I knew
grew completely apart
parted ways parted hearts.

I would write of beauty and not of death
if only I were able.
I would in this day's
black and exact Alaska dawn
be curled fetal still with it all
if death had not
again and again
driven me sleepless from bed.

III

One dead man walking
two dead men dead.
For it was not I
but another
a third man Mike shot
who seemed to have died
under the tucked wings
of chance
a landing swan or a circling falcon
before the stoop,
I ask you who
under the moon and under the sun,
under the great and under the small,

under the smell of the chokecherry tree
and beyond newly feathered duck chicks
paddling with the tiniest
of tiny webbed feet,
able still in the river's current
to follow quacking hens—
will tell me of red iris
who and when?

Under all the beauty
one could dredge up
still a third man died
just because he was there
under the wings of the swan
and under those of death.

IV

When all is said and all is done
below the peaks
and in the valleys
in the Alaska Range,
when all the miners
and all the trappers
and all the guides
below the scissor peaks;
when all the committees
of the mind have met
just where glaciers end
and river's begin;
when all the brown and muddy waters

of the brain begin to flow;
when one of two men I knew
on the banks of Buzzard Creek goes berserk;
when the other with firearms
with witnesses all about
will not back;
when the heat
of the valley's debate
when old and smoldering fires are kindled again
to whom does it all belong
all this beauty of which I could write
but can not
someone kills someone else
again
in the Alaska Range
in beauty's perfect lap
again someone is dead.

VI

I was certain when I learned
two had died
of its certainty
in a horrible way
the prescience of the poet
if not the death of it
the finish of it
like the beauty
of which I can not write
like moss it had grown—
on the north side of knowing.

Here were two men
joined at the hip
one witness said.

Loved the same children and dogs
the same family
the same wilderness, the same fur
the trophies
and the same forest.

We three went up the canyons
and down the winters
went like soldiers
with weapons too
across waist deep rivers
into the trees of the mind
for I was them, and they were me
in my own way attached,
for I knew all they knew
and thought all they thought
and drew them maps of it all
which still exist
with one man living
and two men dead.

VII

I broke bread
with the agony of the beginning
for three hours
with Mike before he killed Ron,
and a third man I did not know
but now somehow do,
for like the circling raven,
and the beauty of which I can not write
to know them each
to be the scribe

is unwanted prey
the poet like the wolf predator too.
Mike sang his song long and sad
the wailing wall of our meeting
my third eye should have seen it—
death grinning in the wilderness.

So a day or two later
when the phone rang
it was a moment
not of beauty
of which I can write
but of death's ill call
announcing yet again
the arrival of so-and-so
to yet another fine ball
death the terrible butler
to the dead their macabre dance.

VIII

It was 2003
the killing done driving free
Mike at Willow Street
a pick-up and a pistol
a rope—
a lost identity.

He had a driver's license
but no where to go
because his mind like that day
like mine today
chose over hope hopelessness.

Inside Ron with a stranger sat
the third man I never knew
but who that day would die
caught in death's crosshairs
when the pick-up was turned off
so was his life.

What happened next
no one knows for sure
but the blue-eyed man
dogs and children and family fled
went armed to death's door
by inhuman fury fed.

One report finds a rope or chain
to the locked door tied
a reigniting of the truck engine
a pulling of the door from its hinges
that single entry and exit
of the little cabin
of whose beauty I can not write.

Through which one man burst
firing if not his weapon
then his agony
while the others inside
in their own right world
made of the debate
as men properly so one to the death.
They shot Mike and Mike shot them
so that Ron fell dead
and the third man too
in similar theme
as Mike brooding and bleeding fled

not on a horse
but in a pick-up
not before the dog
with the other two lay dead
on Willow Street
in Fairbanks in 2003
Mike at large but finally free.

IX

I would write of the color
bee's wings seem to make
if I were able
of pollen's soft and exquisite texture
of a knife blade's perfection
when not too sharp
of how its edge gleams
of how a pistol can do this or do that
but instead here comes death trampling again
its boots on the blossoms of three good men.

I would write of the dog's eyes
when I saw it look at both its masters.
I would wonder at what point
like traps they've set, men's springs snap?

I would wonder where
I shall ever again
know two men
the way I knew them
a dead man walking
and two dead men dead.

X

I would scream of things exquisite—
if I were able
I would write how all the silver stars
and all the glowing and blurring
of the great blue black night
fell like glitter around all we had.

Oh how it streamed over us three!

We showered in it there in the wilderness
in the starlight of the mind pure and clean
bathed in it in every form every day
each day with the sun
our hopes rising like morning breath
made us each and three
take deep breaths and stock repeatedly
beat our chests with a wild and a certain joy
smile and grin with the thrill of it sheepishly
left the forest behind
went sadly and straight to Willow Street
below the landing swan
the circling raven
the diving falcon
those things of beauty
of which I can not write
rather only of arrested men
of a dead man walking
turned himself in
two dead men dead
three now gone—

12-15-03
Fairbanks, AK

OF WAR

Vladimir Mayakovsky

Humans are
advanced machines
winding slowly down
escaping their maker
programmed it seems
like tireless sails on a tireless sea
like them too to self destruct.

We could build humans
I would say
from the black wastes
from the sands and sad nesses
of Mayakovsky's very eyes.

Which saw in 1924
cigarette in hand
quite probably
with humans and humanity in mind
enough by 1930 to shoot himself,
programmed
human—
as he was.

11-23-03
Fairbanks, AK

The Last Drummer Boy

I

God knows
we send them
fife and drum
time and time again
ordinary young men.

God knows
who will be the last
ordinary young man
when red and final blood flow.

God knows
when the time will come
no more sounds
nothing else—
fifeless no more drums.

God knows who will be
the last drummer boy
last alone and last alive
with no one to tell—
will say and see the end
something out there evil reigns.

II

Just past sixteen I went
next to me a boy younger yet
sixty days later
our war ended—
until another began.

We were drummer boys
there in 54
following all
all who had gone before.

We were drummer boys
there in 54
for better men who died
reasonless in other wars.

III

Now we
drummer boys grown old
fifty years from it all in fact
announce anew to new children—
things of quick lightning and of war.

Now we
drummer boys gone
sing loudly our own sunset song
sing purely here sing purely there
all the misery all war would forget.

Once at fifteen sixteen seventeen
we drummed ourselves proudly off to war
in a century gone we pounded our heels
kept sharp time with willful music
and pride fully too to its awful tone.

IV

We were drummer boys
straight-backed children!
And now as old men we cry—
shall we wait for it all to end—
'til *none* are left to die?

Shall the last boy
have no one
spellbound
tales of his own to thrill?

Shall the last boy,
last human alive
search a seamless sky
of war earth to earth
dead to dead
stand with drum sticks—
every possible audience absent
tap a proud and a solo cadence
heed the heels of ghosts
their deaf pounding
tap ever more slowly his quiet little notes
know afterwards then an empty silence
unbroken metal skies
Gods gone mute
then he may cry—
a most horrible shriek.

01-22-04
Gold King, AK

Archimedes

Archimedes three-hundred years before Christ
sliced spheres lifted water with screws
might have reached the moon in 969
but at 32 slain at Syracuse.

Archimedes built machines for war
defense of home and hearth
dead by Roman sword
killed on orders one-thousand years lost
sphere-slicing mind hacked to death—
Archimedes.

He was killed
just beyond being a boy—
we forgot his math
but not how to multiply.

We march ever backward it seems
to caves and clubs and animal skins
to extinguish ourselves not with swords
but with pulpits and populace.

We refuse to embrace
what at birth we know
exchange it all
for war's ugly glow.

09-15-04
Gold King, AK

White Gravestones Line on Line

Words unchecked and evil
carouse about, fall like rain
white gravestones line on line 1917 WWI
warped, strangled, twisted, torn
orphaned from meaning words fall.

Like angry mist on a dark shore they attack
like arguing knives they engrave our minds
white gravestones line on line 1942 WW II
righteously out of the sky words screech
make the roofs shake, the shingles cringe.

Air wave snake oil
hate this whip that
white gravestones line on line 1952 Korea
like tired sailors we bend down
bow to lies dressed as truth.

Worship cloth for cloth's sake
the red white and blue of its wave
gravestones line on line Viet Nam 1967
not the miracle of its weave
chant instead, "My country right or wrong!"

Unchecked and evil rains of it
drown out the once and proud
white gravestones line on line Iraq I 1991
propaganda plain and simple steers us
rudderless on a foul and infected sea.

What of Nuremberg?
What of men in power
white gravestones line on line Iraq II 2001
ordering men who are not, lay their bodies
below white gravestones line on line
tomorrow and tomorrow white gravestones
white by the thousands
line on line
for naught?

04-09-03
Gold King, AK

Galileo, Celeste, and The Patriot Act

First came the Pole Copernicus with the idea,
then Galileo with gall published it,
before the Inquisition at 70 on his knees
Who <u>were they</u>
wedded to a stationary earth?

Galileo's daughter Celeste
secreted her soul in a convent,
camouflaged her intellect
(From Whom?) (God?)
from there aided her father.

It was 1616 Galileo and Celeste did all that
the Dialogs, Shakespeare dying,
The Discourses, physics born
earlier1564
what a time —
what a party —
us, The Church and The Inquisition
ruthlessly murdering thought
as if anything were provable
but thought —
2004 look around
the Patriot Act says
America is the center of the universe.

07-06-04
Fairbanks, AK

The Glory, and The Pain

I

Twice now recently
a vision of Rome
swords helmets armor
shining in sunlight
reflecting glory
of course
and honor
high achievements
of all sort
government
science
art philosophy
a mature society.

Yet mainly
one of marching men
senators in white togas
and over all that
this haunting vision
of America yet to come
Rome again unleashed
a thousand years hence
fresh and healthy.

How proud Italy must be.

II

For me it's the aircraft
two at a time
like two Roman soldiers
patrolling Jerusalem
or the skies
here at home
two aircraft
leave soldier-like foot prints
Romans on patrol
high in the sky immune
young men in armor
doing it again
what young men did then
marching and clanking
through history's dust
breathing it
as if they were the first.

As if we'd invented truth.
The mightier fist always proof.
But last I heard
it hadn't yet been done
not by anyone on this planet
not by Rome
nor by Washington.

III

Rome would civilize
as would we
those with whom
we disagree.

Rome would debate
be diplomatic
as do we
then invade—
after a bow.

Rome went to its limits.
Hadrian built his wall.
Where shall we?

We have gone now twice
circumcising veils
slicing them off
imposing with war peace
as we see it
as King George
until we fought him
unfairly
not on the field
but from hidden places
defending what was ours
from those who would define it for us
who knew better than we
what was
and what ought to be.

IV

We invented something new
and now would impose it
on others too.

We have become British
and the world
has become us.

Twice now
the bird of doom
has called to me
its eerie cry.

I have seen you before
it says,
it calls through the night,
and through the day,
of Rome in homeward retreat
of war planes mute
of wings clipped
of swords broken
of the moral peak
America forgot.

America by a blind dog
led down a sour trail
begins the downward roll
from the long climb up.

V

In armored skirts
the last centurion
turns back his men
on wide roads
leads them to Rome.

As they did then
so shall we now.

So all this I see
out here in the wilderness
as above me a new Rome soars
brave and pure
to somewhere—
they can not know.

Who is to say
what they believed then
those fine men
armed and Roman
brave and human—
what ours believe now?

I shall say it
for Rome
and for them too,
for ours.

It is the glory
and too the pain.

Brave
we have all and each
made clear.
Of brave we have proof.

If pure we once possessed
today it avoids us, and neatly so
for pure is not nearly so easy we see
say—
as bravery to achieve.

Pure is impossible,
for us it would seem,
from this summit we occupy
label it The High Moral Peak,
as in, what we say or think is right,
and what you say and think is not,
then begin our attacks—
we the Romans, the British
the Americans—
from this mountain to which
each have laid claim
though none its final top—
has ever attained.

06-24-03
Gold King, AK

OF HUMANITY

Francisco Pessoa

His sky brightens with dangerous gifts
Pessoa bequeaths manna from heaven
relentless child he bears strict news
sticks to me like a primitive magnet
forces clouds before my eyes
in mid-stride to halt
waterfalls too in his child's eye
which we at once with laughter—
us praise and slaughter
like a solid plank of Serra's bed
Pessoa in all this blackness
is a candle's flame.

Pessoa one more little laborer
Emily, Sylvia, Serra, Lorca
keepers each of precious sheep
in them our best thoughts escape the prison
their bloodied fingers our barbed wire
in Portuguese and in Spanish
in small and distant rooms they scribbled
in Boston, Lisbon, London, Castile, Gold Stream
far and far away—
might as well have been off the planet.

12-18-03
Gold King, AK

Dandelions

Their roots are deep, tenacious
treacherous in survival
break when pulled
grow again
thicker, deeper still
little yellow flowers
unyielding and complex
in Seldovia six feet tall
it seemed
adapting
to taller grasses
grew taller yet
became sun flowers
a sea of them
are the enemy
in old age I choose
for the peace their death delivers
in *The Onion Field*—
from the battles
life does not.

Fairbanks, AK
06-18-04

The Maypole Dance

Life now
is not the maypole season,
the one we once knew,
ring-around-the-rosie
floating iridescent gleaming
pocket-full-of-posies
all-fall-down
all-fall-down
now we neither float nor gleam
instead
becoming again children
olly-olly-oxen-free
neighborhood shades get pulled down
social codes slam shut on us like cell doors
three-blind-mice
three-blind-mice
while secretly unspeakably
we search in dull ways for places to die
perhaps a burial at sea?
see-how-they-run
see-how-they-run
or in the forest in the bear's embrace
they-all-ran-after-the-farmer's-wife
but never we pray
who-cut-off-their-tale's
with-a-carving-knife
alone in a hotel room—

11-18-03
Fairbanks, AK

A Penguin On The March

Though untouched
I am a crippled king of what I own
traded castles
faith for faith
out in the depths
I play on
further and further
farther and farther
carefully now with my pawns
one precious step at a time
into the deep —
to the board's far and black side
pieces missing
continuing awkwardly
a penguin on the march
for somewhere out there
in the last row waiting
there the queen exists
for those of us —
yet arriving.

11-10-03
Gold King, AK

The Savage Poem Which Rules

I gave my twenty minutes of poem reading
of oh-three to Serge and Miles
in exchange
for a summer solo—
being dared to gather a crowd.

If you've been where I've been
or probably Serge and Miles too
it is not the crowd by any means
but the savage poem
which rules.

I've neither met
nor their poems much read,
remain sure
they would read to blank walls
and empty rooms
if that's all they had.

I'll give it to you straight
and to the arts association too
we do not write for crowds
or for the king of England
but because we have no choice
in it—
or the manner of our deaths.

11-05-03
Fairbanks, AK

A Public Dancing Of The Mind

Life ought not leak away
like water in old buckets,
better brashly fled
cascading outward
a public dancing of the mind.

First breath to last
on this round and odd place
life ought not to go stale—
be passionless
ought better order itself
march to a foreign legion of dreams
give itself to answers
 if need be—
escape cities.

More even—
so perturbed I persist.
Portuguese to navigate
beyond the dullness of answers even.

Instead to the on and on
where at last I will sit myself
upon a boulder upon a shore
of a dreadful and a final sea.
There will be a beach of silver and torn sand
where with strands of wet and twisted seaweed
I will spell it out: all the where and all the why?

07-11-04
Gold King, AK
(For Pete, who seeks.)

A Ladder Of Haiku

There has to be a way
to learn the Morse code
of the universe.
To make it all work.

Preamble aside
unequivocally I venture
the Morse code
of the universe is music.

So the closer poems come
to being tapping, little-keyed songs
"Strange harmonies"
someone once said
"A weird musical cadence"
someone else offered,
then the closer poems move
to where ever we are going.

Of course I shout!
For the further we move
from where ever we are,
the closer we come
to a ladder of haiku
up and up
the white and glowing sides.

08-31-03
Fairbanks

The Uncaptured Brain

Safe to think
we assume
okay
just nothing.

But it was not good for Rimbaud
nor Good Tom
nor Plath
nor Schandelmeirer
whoever else?

The uncaptured brain
is an unsafe place.

Absent inspiration
the think machine
bounces fruitless
off the walls.

Straight jackets I always thought
even they had good purpose.

Lead for the Romans,
sloth and plenty
for Americans.

03-03-03
Fairbanks, AK

In Wilder Fields Still

The soul not the brain
pulls from the weave
of what we see
from the threads of what is
wheat from chaff
faith from fact
Thomas and I.

God, Job said
separated sea from sky
earth from wisdom
hid faith's Easter egg
for us to find.

I find myself then
swimming if not beside Job
nor with Darwin either firmly,
but pursuing with all and each of them
the magnificent IT
in wilder fields still
for I am human
a tuning fork
for I here sir
only to measure secret tones
sift starlight
and naught from naught
vibrating not fraudulent
I go to a places
which wait for us still—
so you may too.

12-07-03
Fairbanks, AK

Haiku

#1

Long necked swans wide winged
silvery arrows of light
point wonderfully.

10/15/03

#2

Dark steep-ridged mountains
they call like winter's doorway
to a long night's sleep.

10/16/03

#3

Autumn leaves brown and falling
The gentle snow imparts
A roof for dreams.

10/17/03

#4

Distant Summers Call
Pleading For Our Tolerance
Wild Flowers Grow Strong.

10-19-03

#5

October's death sings
carols of the hermit thrush
soothing our anguish.

10/20/03

#6

Mists of winter's night
live once moving perfectly
and wraith-like vanish.

10/21/03

#7

Sere and yellow leaves
sienna fields call me home
winter is death's brief.

10/21/03

#8

Scarlet maples die
brightness falling on brown earth
Ceres weeps once more.

10-21-03

The Peacock's Truth

A black man sees me white
criminal
I see a black man black
criminal
we have each ungodlike built
thorough architects which we are
jointly an eloquent cage
deaf and dumb itself
a gray and horrible prison
no matter where our houses are
it races us through a life of days
their exact length and width
predetermined left and right
back and forth each day
we pace our terrible cages—
absent the peacock's truth.

01-26-04
Fairbanks, AK

Idiots

Idiots see
right through walls
to other places
perhaps to conclusions
requiring neither alphabet nor math
as we know them
to spell the names of what they see
so instead they mime
with their eyes into mine
dig in moments with sharp daggers
deep pits into my soul
between drops of thorazine
through the bars of tiny openings
belted from their cells.

And so our guards watch them
as did I
our straight-jacketed folk —
profoundly I would hope
as did I.

05-11-04
Gold King, AK

Christer In Palm Springs

We spotted him together
Marilyn and I foreigners in Palm Springs
from our rental auto
with street maps
the new rules of every town.

Christ there with a lawnmower—
made us speechless
or was he just another nude gardener
one or the other—
was there a third choice?

He came right at us
as we studied street maps
down the sidewalk
barefoot, marching it seemed
determined in the evening's dusk
to be stalwart
and on by us—
mowing cement and completely naked
the grassless sidewalks of Palm Springs
gave us both the full-fore-and-aft
the full poem of all human hair
the full song of all human parts
with some odd power
possessed of a mower
its churning and its clanking
its utility—
if nothing more.

12-30-03
Gold King, AK

Ballet

The body springs free of itself
becomes something more
possesses certain majesty
motion wildly successful
makes our of silence sound
stories
knees alliterative
right angled ankles
a precise architecture
an imitation of some action
hidden
unexplained—
drunken even in some kind of odd joy
soberly—
we call it—
ballet.

08-10-04
Gold King, AK

The Bookcase

There is a weak and leaning bookcase
outside
ought to go to the dumps
but it hides
in a corner of my life
refuses to just go away!

I place a book in it
Hiroshima adjacent to
The Life Of Mother Theresa
The Bible by Mein Kampf
this poem next to your brain.

10-22-04
Fairbanks, AK

Before I Was Born

Birds of gray swamp stone
lily pads in ponds which dance
I pursue them as others have
Spanish poets and Portuguese.

The darkest of dark frontiers
the windiest of windy plains
the furthest of far fields
the last and final star
those I claim and those are mine.

Off even this round earth
not to know its circle —
but more its' why?
Quem passar o Cabo de Nam
ou tornara ou nam.

No one I know has brought it back whole
so it's all we have here I choose to leave
and with the mind's careful fission
swim strongly in days yet to come
through wilder seas and stormier skies
to a last and final land where light was lit
and there build a windjammer of poems
sail seriously about and wake and know
for my ticket was purchased
ere a wave knew motion or a leaf fell
far and far before I was born
that deed was done.

05-07-04
Gold King, AK

"These poems capture the gusto of those who love Alaska beyond streets and phones and desks…", **Anchorage Times.**

"…America's leading wilderness poet." **E-Bay**

"Charming, educated and natural…" <u>Messages</u> <u>From</u> <u>Raven</u> in **Envoy.**

"If Not For The Owl At Night…strikes me as a perfect poem." Tom Sexton, Alaska Poet Laureate

"He took me to the wilderness…couldn't help but feel both the healing and vast aloneness of the wilds." **Robin W. Westerville, OH.**   <u>Messages</u> <u>From</u> <u>The</u> <u>Bombing</u> <u>Range</u>

"…read and digested each poem like a good meal for the soul." **Phyllis T. Highland, CA.**   <u>Bombing</u> <u>Range</u>

"Honest prose, excellent style." **Mark M. Rock Point, AZ**

"Captures the still vastness of winter…the fragility of life on the tundra…solitude at the top of the world…stark…a great volume." **Ryan M. Pacific Grove, CA**. <u>Messages</u> <u>From</u> <u>The</u> <u>Bombing</u> <u>Range.</u>

"…beautiful…lyrical…I could smell the trees…felt the anguish and pain of learning…" **Patricia M. Fort Worth, TX**

"Too short…wanted to read more of these inspirational words."
"Messages From The Bombing Range"
Valarie T. London, ON Canada.

"…these poems come from the heart…nothing in the book I did not like." **Kristine N. E. Falmouth, MA**

"Thoroughly enjoyed reading…thought provoking…well written…I wanted more of it. BUY THE BOOK!"
Tom M. Brookings, OR

"I love the poetry. Wonderful stories…an unexpected pleasure…wished it was longer."
Linda E. Wrens, GA

"This book has great enthusiasm and energy…enchants with its melodic rhythms."
Adam H. Louisville, KY

"Amazing images…the author put himself into these poems."
Casey K. South Beach, OR

"Wonderful descriptions…made you feel like you were there."
Kristina C. Huntersville, NC

www.ingramcontent.com/pod-product-compliance
Lightning Source LLC
Chambersburg PA
CBHW020259290526
45784CB00003B/1303